TOPSHAM SAGA

ARMADA AND

SHIP OWNERS

APSAM BOOKS of TOPSHAM

TOPSHAM SAGA: THE ARMADA
AND SHIP OWNERS

© 1994   Sadru Bhanji
         Illustrations by Jan M. Rogers

ISBN   1 874461 05 8

All rights reserved. No part of this publication may be reproduced, stored in a retrieval system, transmitted in any form by any means electrical, mechanical or photocopied, recorded or otherwise without prior permission of the publishers.

British Library Cataloguing–in–Publication Data:
A catalogue record for this book is available from the British Library.

Library of Congress:
Registration pending.

TO Helen Raddon, Robert Raddon, Riannon Cheffers–Heard, Lee Rogers, Jonathan and Laura Sprague, Jessica and Nathaniel May, Martyn and Charlotte Gill, Amy Louise Llewellyn and the other young people of TOPSHAM.

Published and printed by Apsam Books of Topsham
Covers printed by Optima Graphics of Topsham

AD 1580 to 1625

CONTENTS

Illustrations **4**

What and When? **4**

Introduction **5**

1. Across the Atlantic to fish **7**
2. Pirates or patriots? **11**
3. The Armada **19**
4. Tudor farming **27**
5. Merchant families **31**
6. The Elizabethan maid **40**
7. The poor and the law **47**

Appendices:
  I. Chronology **52**
  II. Notes and summary of sources **53**

Acknowledgements **55**

Note: Book 22 contains a full list of sources referenced to key words in each page of books in the series.

TOPSHAM SAGA - 6

ILLUSTRATIONS

Cover: An English galleon drawn by Janet Rogers; and the seal is that of the Peculiar of Topsham.
Lead page: the schooner *Racer*.

1 A conjectured impression of *Whitt Beare*. **9**
2 A 16th century impression of a galleass with oars. **10**
3 An impression of the Tayllours' fortified farm. **17**
4 The pinnace *Gyfte of God* ... in the 1580s. **18**
5 A cannon in the Spanish fleet. **21**
6 Entry in Chamber records ... to Nicholas Spicer... **25**
7 A Tudor breakfast and main meal... **28**
8 Principal members of the Spicer family. **32**
9 Wear House in the Tudor period ... **33**
10 Spicers' staple marks identifying their goods. **34**
11 Tudor playing cards. **41**
12 A vagrant of Tudor times. **48**

WHAT AND WHEN?

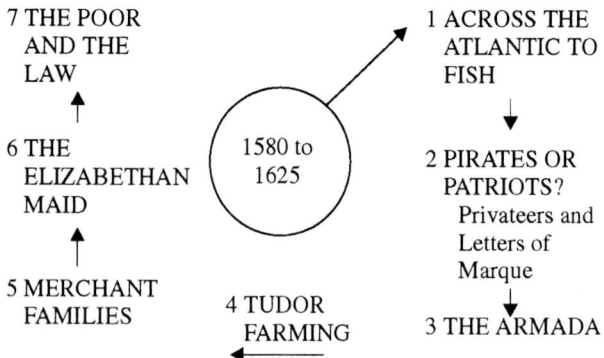

4

AD 1580 to 1625

INTRODUCTION

1580 was the 23rd year of Queen Elizabeth's reign (note 1). She was an energetic ruler, revered by most of her subjects but feared and respected by her enemies and the politically ambitious. In many aspects she appears to have acquired the better features of her father's personality. However, unlike Edward VI and Mary I there is no evidence that she inherited his syphilis. She gave her name to the Elizabethan era, which has been described as one of heroes and adventurers. Heroism, however, was often tinged with villainy and those who travelled afar were by no means all altruistic geographers and missionaries. Their main motive would seem to have been the acquisition of wealth. Nevertheless, their actions often called for great courage. Some, such as Sir Humphrey Gilbert who drowned in 1583 after establishing a settlement in Newfoundland, paid dearly.

Elizabeth I inherited large debts. Careful management helped by the ability to raise money at favourable rates of interest improved matters, as did trade with Spain and the Netherlands. By 1580 England's economy was booming, enabling capital to be provided for ship building and merchant ventures. Both these activities would have benefitted Topsham. There was more work for its shipwrights, and its seamen would sail to the profitable cod fishing grounds off Newfoundland or fetch tobacco and sugar from the West Indies.

War with Spain brought a temporary halt to this prosperity and the thoughts of the people of Topsham would have been turned away from peaceful trading. When the Armada threatened to land an invading army in 1588, Topsham men and ships were to sail in support of Howard and Drake. Those left behind had their different battles to fight. Topsham was not only a port, but also a farming community. In Tudor times much livestock was to fall prey to disease.

The everyday life of the comfortably well off of Topsham would have been less complicated than it is today. This may have been due to the robust and at times unsubtle way in which day–by–day problems were dealt with. The poor, by contrast, had much harshness to contend with, but the various Poor Laws were to lay the foundations of the modern welfare state.

When Elizabeth I died in 1603 England's standing in the world was high. She was succeeded by James VI of Scotland, who became James I of England, the first of the Stuart monarchs. He lacked Elizabeth's dynamism and appears to have been content to let the country rest on its laurels. In spite of its proven value, he allowed the navy to decline. Topsham men were to be among those who then fell into the hands of pirates. In 1625 the crown passed to Charles I. His stubbornness and lack of tact were to ensure that Topsham men would again bear arms. This time, however, the threat was to be from their own countrymen.

It is inevitable that money will be mentioned a good deal in a book which concerns farmers, merchants and the poor. Those unfamiliar with pre–decimal currency will find details of this so–called L–S–D (£:s:d with £ for *Libra* a pound sterling, s for shilling and d for *denarius* penny) in Appendix II of Book 5.

Sadru Bhanji
October 1994

AD 1580 to 1625

1 ACROSS THE ATLANTIC TO FISH

Newfoundland was discovered in 1497 by John Cabot, an Italian who had settled in Bristol. Its rich cod fishing grounds were soon exploited by Portuguese, Bretons and Normans. English seamen, however, had adequate inshore catches and obtained sufficient cod off Iceland, only visiting on a regular basis until the middle of the 16th century. Among the first ships to sail for Newfoundland from the Exe were the *Whitt Beare* and the *Trenite* of Topsham.

The *Whitt Beare*
The *Whitt Beare* sailed from the Exe estuary in October 1582 carrying goods to the West Indies before going on to Newfoundland. She was owned by Thomas Spicer (see Chapter 5) in partnership with her master who lived at nearby Lympstone. The cargo was in part provided by Spicer. Her departure was later in the year than usual, but the *Whitt Beare* was a well-found ship of 120 tuns burden and her master was apparently prepared to brave the winter Atlantic storms. She was back in the Exe estuary by September of the following year bringing cod from Newfoundland and probably rum and sugar from the Caribbean. Few merchants were interested only in fish, and in Devon preferred to operate a free enterprise system rather than as members of such large concerns as existed in Bristol and London.

The Topsham 'bankers'
Many more Topsham ships would bring back fish from the shores and Grand Banks of Newfoundland. By the 1650s the town had the largest English fleet apart from that of London. Their voyages

were long and arduous. The ships would usually set out in February or March and reach the fishing grounds some three months later. There they would stay until August. At first, fish were caught by rod and line from the beaches or from small inshore boats. Later, nets were to be used over the banks themselves. To begin with the cod were preserved in salt and shipped back as 'green' cod. By the end of the 16th century, however, the English in particular were drying fish on especially constructed platforms. This meant that the men had to spend more time ashore. As well as bringing them into contact with the native people, this increased any quarrelling between different fleets. Discipline among the English was enforced by the Fishing Admiral, the first captain to arrive each spring. He had first choice of location for his shore premises, and authority over other ships who came into his particular harbour. The second captain into harbour became the vice–admiral and the third the rear–admiral.

On their homeward voyage many ships would put in at the Canaries or at Mediterranean ports. Back in the Exe some captains preferred unloading from the deep waters off Starcross, but others sailed on to Topsham. Cod unloaded there was then taken to Exeter by packhorse. Not all ships who failed to return were lost to pirates or the gales and storms of the Atlantic. In 1573 the unfortunate *John* of Lympstone was wrecked in the estuary due to the 'craft, fault, ignorance, rashness and negligence of the pilot'.

Spain withdraws
Towards the end of the 16th century the major Newfoundland fishing fleets were those of England, France and Spain. In 1585, however, the last of these virtually disappeared. Their King, Philip II, had judged that his ships and sailors were better employed in preparing for an invasion of England.

AD 1580 to 1625

1 *A conjectured impression of* Whitt Beare.

TOPSHAM SAGA - 6

2 *A 16th century impression of a galleass with oars.*

2 PIRATES OR PATRIOTS?

War and weather were not the only hazards to those who went to sea. Pirates would also account for many lost cargoes and lives. Generations ago the Veneti might have sold into slavery any Celtic seaman whom these Britanny seafarers captured after he had sailed from the Eisca estuary. In a later age Saxon pirates put to death many of their captives. The Vikings posed a double danger as they plundered both on land and at sea. The cramped conditions on their longships meant that few if any men were taken alive. After the Norman conquest independent pirate captains, whose ships might shelter in some quiet bay in the Channel Islands, roamed the seas.

Held to ransom
Piracy had consequences over and above losses of men, ships and cargo. In 1483, after the *Le Anne* of Topsham had been captured by Brittany pirates, Richard III had to grant £40 from the customs and tolls of Exeter and Dartmouth toward the crew's ransom. This was £130 which her owners Ralph Bukland and John Langley had undertaken to pay for the release of her crew of 52 men. In later years, however, it became more usual for ransoms to be raised by church or door-to-door collections, or to be dealt with by the Quarter Sessions.

Privateers and Letters of Marque
During wartime, ship captains could be granted a 'letter of marque' by their Duke or King which licensed them to prey on a specified enemy. Many of these privateers abused this authority and plundered when and where the opportunity presented. In 1386

a privateer captain seized a ship and her cargo, which he then claimed to be French. The prize was taken to Topsham, where it was discovered that the ship was owned by a Southampton merchant. Richard II ordered the agent of the Admiral of the West, the Earl of Devon, to look into the matter, but it appears to have taken some time for the merchant to have his goods returned, if he ever did.

Two years later, in 1388, Richard II again had reason to question the Admiral. Two ships laden with salt had been arrested by the Earl and were being held in Topsham and Fowey (Cornwall). The salt was said to be the property of a Paris merchant, John Englisshe, described as a rebel. The king asked for further information and that it be established whether or not the salt should now be his. Another incident involving salt took place some years later in 1546, but this time the authorities looked kindly on the matter. A cargo of salt landed at Topsham was exempted from paying duty before the cargo was unloaded, as the vessel carrying it was leaking badly.

There were also other occasions when kings regretted the enthusiasm of their privateers. In 1445 a Frenchman, Peter Claver of Poitiers, complained that his ship had been taken when approaching Topsham. Although a treaty existed he had been placed in prison and his cargo confiscated. In 1546, in order that another treaty might not be jeopardised, a ship and a barque belonging to John Malyn of Calais, then English territory, were forbidden to leave Topsham with their cargoes until he had given an undertaking not to molest the French.

Morality was not the only matter to concern the enquiries into alleged piracy. Ownership of the prize and any liability to duty had also to be established. In some cases the matter could not be easily resolved. In 1545 the Mayor of Topsham was instructed to allow the *Santo Christophano* to set sail with her cargo, but to hold himself accountable if within eight months it turned out to belong to the French. In the reign of Charles I the *Endeavour* of Topsham, acting under letter of marque, took the Spanish *Nostra Seniora de Candelarea* carrying tobacco and sugar from Brazil. It was agreed this was a lawful prize, but the owner of the *Endeavour* was nevertheless made to pay duty.

In 1627 John Nutt brought into Topsham a captured Portugese ship carrying sugar and treasure said to value £10,000, and Captain William Carey a French vessel laden with fish. The Mayor of Exeter and a notary, Walter Sainthill, were both censured for disposing of the prizes without any authority from the Court of Admiralty. Another dispute over a prize took place in 1629. The *Willing Minde* of Topsham had captured the *Nostra Seniora de Bona Franca* bound from Brazil with a cargo of sugar. It was alleged that the owners, possibly in collusion with the master Stephen Taylor, had swindled the crew out of their share of the £17,000 prize money. Taylor may have been a member of a Topsham family whose exploits had earned them much notoriety a century and a half beforehand.

The Tayllours of Topsham
In 1484 a ship belonging to a Britanny merchant, Nicholas Codelam, of Morlaix set sail for Topsham carrying a cargo of Aquitaine wines, oil, linen cloths and other goods intended as the ransom to release Bretons captured during the recent war between England and France. In spite of having letters of safe conduct, the ship was seized by three ships led by Richard Tayllour of Topsham. The king ordered that restitution be made and that the guilty be arrested. Richard Tayllour had already caused concern by taking a departing ship the same year in order to hold the crew to ransom. He was probably the same Richard Tayllour who in 1467 had been charged with evading duty on a cargo he exported to St

Malo. In 1482 he was pardonned for various misdeeds, but this excluded any debts owed to the Crown.

Having had no response to a previous order Richard III wrote in 1485 asking for a second enquiry into the allegation by Gilaim Marcellis, a subject of the Duke of Austria, that a John Tayllour had unlawfully captured one of his ships. As one Richard Tayllour was one of those conducting the enquiry, it is doubtful if the outcome was particularly helpful.

The Tayllour family lived for generations in a fortified farmhouse at what is now the corner of Follett Road and Fore Street, and at one time leased the Quay. During the early 16th century Peter Tayllour, described as a Topsham merchant, and a John Tayllour, a yeoman, were sued for debts but appear to have been uncooperative with the authorities. Later that century, a John Tayler (sic) took on the name John Thomas when he was pursued for money owing. However, his alias was yet to acquire its present slang meaning. Station Road was once known as Taylor's Lane and Hannaford's Quay was at one time Taylor's Quay.

William Hull of Topsham

A later Topsham pirate who managed to keep in favour with the authorities is William Hull of the *Dolphin* (also known as the *Talbot*). Towards the end of Queen Elizabeth's reign he and others had taken iron, ship's gear, catapults and accessories from a French vessel, the *Serena*. In 1607 he was pardonned and it was requested that leniency be shown regarding any pending and future proceedings.

John Nutt of Lympstone

The John Nutt referred to above was another pirate based on the Exe. On one occasion he and some Turks chased an English man–of–war into harbour. On another, he captured Lord

Wentworth's luggage, furniture, wardrobe and plate while it was on its way to Ireland where Wentworth was about to become Lord Deputy. In a later exploit he is said to have seized a ten-gunned Exeter vessel lying in the estuary, while her crew were resting ashore.

The Dunkirkers

The English did not always have matters their own way when dealing with the French. Towards the end of the 16th century the Merchant Adventurers of Exeter (see chapter 5) were sufficiently troubled by French pirates, sailing mainly out of Dunkirk, that they considered avoiding France altogether and trading instead with Guernsey and Jersey. In 1578 they had asked the Queen for a ship to protect the coasts of Devon and Cornwall and sent £100 to defray any expenses. This was not provided, but she gave permission for Exeter to have its own warship with the same powers and privileges as hers.

The Turks

Up to the beginning of the 17th century losses of shipping were to European pirates and usually confined to times of war. The main threat was now to come from North Africa. Although referred to as 'Turks', most of these pirates sailed from Algiers or the Moroccan port of Salee.

They operated in well organised fleets between April and October, preying mainly on West Country seamen. Coastal towns were rife with tales of their cruelty toward Christians. It was rumoured that they cut out the tongues of those they did not kill, or lopped off the ears and forced the victim to eat them. In fact, most captives were taken intact to North Africa where they waited to be ransommed or sold as slaves. In spite of many entreaties the government was slow to respond, pleading at first a lack of ships and then dismissing the fears of the West Country as panic and hysteria.

Ineffectual measures
In 1565 a Privy Council order was made for the repression of pirates. Commissioners were appointed with powers to ensure that Deputies, drawn from 'honeste, discrete and trustye persons' were available to inspect incoming and out going shipping. No ship was to go to sea without the permission of the Deputies, and if armed should carry only sufficient guns for its defence. The carriage of 'victual, leather, horses, mares or geldings' also required a license, and grain required a royal warrant. The Deputies were empowered to remove and sell offending cargoes, and could arrest suspicious persons. They were not to provide victuals unless for 'good and true merchants' or 'honest passengers'. As with other measures this proved largely ineffectual. The problem of piracy was not to be tackled with any real success until the days of Cromwell. Letters of marque continued to be issued, and continued to be abused. Privateering, both from Topsham and elsewhere, was to reach its heyday in the 18th century and is reviewed further in book 10.

AD 1580 to 1625

3 *An impression of the Tayllours' fortified farm.*

TOPSHAM SAGA - 6

4 *The pinnace* Gyfte of God *as she probably appeared in the 1580s, pinnaces had the general appearance of galleons but were small with all guns on the upper deck.*

AD 1580 to 1625

3 THE ARMADA

The seamanship learned during the hazardous voyage to Newfoundland and back were soon to stand England in good stead. In spite of their previous friendship, animosity had built up between Elizabeth, whom many saw as the natural leader of the European Protestants, and Philip II of Spain. He regarded himself as the champion of the Catholic faith. There was also the matter of England's mariners breaking the Spanish monopoly of trade and treasure. In 1585 Philip arranged for grain to be bought over from England, the Spanish harvest having been poor. In spite of a promise of safety, the ships were seized and their crews placed in prison. The *Primrose*, of London, managed to escape and brought back a number of Spanish captives as well as some incriminating documents.

Preparations for War
Francis Drake was ordered to rescue as many of the English as he could and then to cause chaos in the Spanish West Indies. This retribution, however, did nothing to deter Philip's aim of restoring Catholicism to England. By the time Drake had returned to Plymouth the Spaniards were building a large fleet, the Armada, to carry an invading army from the Netherlands. The Marquis de Santa Cruz was to command the 130 or so ships, and the Duke of Parma the army.

Thanks to Sir Francis Walsingham's extensive network of spies, the English were well aware of these preparations. Drake persuaded Elizabeth I to allow him to strike before the Spaniards were ready to sail. His fleet sailed in April 1587 to Cadiz and destroyed some 24 large vessels, including the flagship. Stores held on shore were also disposed of. The final blow was the capture of £114,000 worth of treasure on its way to Spain.

On his return Drake discovered that policy had changed. Ships had been laid up and their crews sent home. Fortunately for England, Santa Cruz postponed the invasion until after the winter gales. During that winter he died and was succeeded reluctantly by the Duke of Medina Sidonia. The army of 16,000 men grew weary of waiting in the Netherlands and many deserted. Others died of fever or starvation. On the other hand, preparations went well in England. Munitions factories were set up and an army was raised to defend London. Coastal defences were established, Sir Walter Raleigh and Sir Richard Grenville being placed in charge of Devon and Cornwall.

Apsam ships
The navy also needed reinforcing, and on 3 April 1588 the Queen wrote to various coastal towns. Her demands included two ships and a pinnace from Exeter and Apsam (Topsham) to join Drake in Plymouth by 25 April. After much evasiveness and vacillation on the part of the Exeter Chamber, and a stern reminder from Walsingham, the *Rose*, the *Bartholomew* and the *Gyfte of God* were provided. Their departure, however, was further delayed by the weather and they did not arrive at Plymouth until over two months later than ordered. A fourth ship had volunteered for service and had sailed on 13 June. This was the 100 tun *Grace of God*, owned and captained by Walter Edney.

The *Rose*, a ship of 110 tuns which was to carry 50 men was owned by Nicholas Spicer and William Brailie and captained by Thomas Sandye. Spicer was Sheriff of Exeter and perhaps felt obliged to send one of his own ships. The 130 tun *Bartholomew* is said to have been owned by a member of the Raleigh family and carried 70 men under Nicholas Wright. Both these ships

AD 1580 to 1625

would already have been armed. This was necessary if hostile vessels were to be dealt with on the long Atlantic voyages. The 25 tun pinnace the *Gyfte of God* was owned by Thomas Spicer and Abraham Coombes, her usual master. She would have required both strengthening and arming if her crew of twenty were to be of any value.

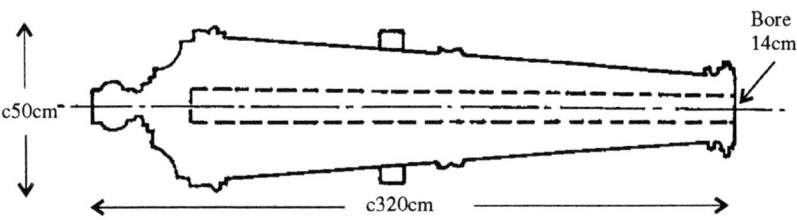

5 *A cannon in the Spanish fleet, 1588.*

On 29 April, the day before they were due to sail, the City Chamber ordered that £250 be paid to the owners of the *Rose* and 200 marks to Thomas Spicer and Abraham Coombes. Five days later more money was required for victualling as the ships had been unable to leave port. Sixteen pounds was granted to the *Gyfte of God* and £30 to the *Rose*. Over a month later the Apsam fleet had still not left and money was needed for the crews' wages. The Chamber agreed that £23 be given to the owners of the Bartholomew. Those of the *Rose* received £17:10:0, the owners of the pinnace £7.

Eventually the weather eased, and the Apsam ships joined Drake at Plymouth on around 16 July. Conditions on board would have been grim. All three vessels carried more men than usual. Accommodation would have been cramped, and the crews' discomfort increased by wood smoke from galley fires built below

21

decks over the ballast. There was also the stench from the tubs of urine held ready in case of fire. Life on the Spanish ships was also harsh. When the captured galleon the *Nuestra Senora del Rosario* was brought to Torbay her crew was close to starvation. Their fish had gone rotten and their bread was full of worms.

The Armada
The Armada sailed from Lisbon in May 1588, but soon had to seek shelter from storms. The fleet finally left Corunna on 12 July. A week later its sighting off the Lizard was reported to Lord Howard of Effingham and to Drake, his Vice–Admiral. Most reports state that this was by Thomas Fleming whose *Golden Hind* had been sailing under orders to watch for the approach of the enemy. One tradition, however, suggests that it was a Topsham privateer who carried the news after being fired at by the Spaniards. He managed to land in Cornwall and then travelled speedily to Plymouth. Another story is that the Commodore of the Newfoundland fishing fleet, Richard Whitbourne of what in the 1990s is Exmouth, heard of the Armada and ordered the ships back to Devon to offer their service to Drake. They reached Plymouth just before the Spanish fleet was in sight.

The English sailed forth the next day and tacked in line to windward to harass the Spanish fleet, which in keeping with its military approach to naval warfare was in crescent formation. The Spaniards rallied and gathered in. Howard then broke off the attack, but was later able to take advantage of an explosion aboard one of the Spanish ships, the *San Salvador*. At the end of the day both fleets hove to off Plymouth, having caused each other little damage. English ammunition and powder, however, were running low.

Early the next morning the Armada set off toward the Isle of Wight, followed by Howard. By evening the south–west wind had dropped and both fleets were becalmed beyond Portland Bill (Dorset). Another battle took place, during which the fleets drifted back toward Lyme Bay. On 23 July an offshore north–east wind gave the Spaniards the advantage. An engagement took place, but again ended in stalemate. Similar operations were repeated the next day when, because of the lack of wind, some of the English ships had to be towed into battle by the oarsmen in the ships' boats. For two more days the fleets drifted eastwards on light south–west winds and by the evening of 26 July were off Calais. The Apsam ships were presumably with the English squadrons, acting as supply vessels, but it is not possible to even conjecture their routes.

Medina Sidonia then discovered that there was no deep anchorage on the Flemish coast. To add to his problems, Parma was not ready to embark his army and doubted the safety of his troop–carrying barges. The coast had been watched and menaced by Dutch 'Sea Beggars' (note 2), and a small English fleet had been patrolling for some time.

On 28 July Howard had little option but to send in his fire–ships (note 3).They breached the defending line of pinnaces and caused havoc. Perhaps exhilarated by this, Howard set off in pursuit of a galleass. Drake, however, kept a clear head and led his ships down on a south–west wind to attack the Spaniards before they could regroup. The battle lasted some eight hours, during which the wind veered north–west and placed the Armada in further danger from prowling Sea Beggars and the hazards of the Dutch coast. Spain lost 600 men in the engagement and over 800 were wounded. The English lost no ships and only 25 men.

On 30 July, as the English were closing in for the kill, a squall set in and the wind backed into the south–west enabling Medina Sidonia to escape into open sea. The English set off in pursuit and on 2 August were off Newcastle upon Tyne. The wind turned north–west, but the Spanish fleet ignored this opportunity to attack. A gale then caused both fleets to shelter where they could. Most of the Armada, however, struggled on its way home round the far northern isles of Scotland and the west coast of Ireland. Many Spanish ships were wrecked and their crews taken captive or slaughtered. In some respects the English fared little better. Thousands died of food poisoning or fever during their long wait to be paid off.

What of the Apsam ships?
The four vessels were discharged from service to Her Majesty on 9 September. The *Gyfte of God* had sailed for St Malo the day before, and the *Grace of God* was to leave for Le Havre by way of Newhaven on 25 September. Nothing is known of the further voyages of the *Bartholomew* or the *Rose*. It appears, however, that all the crews were paid promptly by their owners. In Exeter even the masters who had not made the voyage were compensated, Abraham Coombes receiving £82:13:4. The Spicers and Walter Edney paid off their crews and sought reimbursement of their expenses. These included 14/– per month wages for each man and a similar sum for victuals. The owners' charge for the use of their ships was 2/– per ton per month. The total cost of the three vessels provided by the City Chamber amounted to £447:16:0. The Spicers apparently soon received their money, but the owner of the *Bartholomew* had to complain to Walsingham about the tardiness of the Chamber. Edney no doubt experienced even greater delay as the Privy Council were responsible for the £88:10:0 due for providing, manning and fitting out the *Grace of God*.

The benefits of the English victory were political rather than economic. Apart from some profit from privateering, the defeat of the Armada did little to swell Elizabeth's coffers. Parsimony

> *Decimo septimo die Junii ... 1588*
> *... it is agreed that there should be paid to John Dier towards the pqymt of waige of the men of the Bartholomewe £23:0:0 Also to Mr Nicholas Spicer and William Brayley for waige of the men in the Rose £17:18:8 and to Mr Thomas Spicer for the waiges of the men of the pynnes £7:0:0 ...*

6 *Entry in Chamber records of sums paid to Nicholas Spicer for his ship which sailed against the Armada. The original is in a spidery writing difficult to read, with spellings as above.*

still had to be the order of the day. A typical example was the months it took Edney to get a worn 10–inch rope replaced.

Later Armadas
A second Armada set sail for England in 1596. As it did so in November, it is not surprising that the fleet was wrecked by storms before losing sight of the Spanish coastline. In 1597 the third Armada came close to success, but succumbed to a northerly gale as it approached Falmouth. The fourth Armada set out not for England, but to reinforce the Spanish army in Flanders. It was able to reach Calais undetected by the English fleet.

Only his death, in 1598, ended Philip's aim to conquer England. There were many others in Spain, however, who wished to rid the English of Protestantism. A seaman reached Topsham in 1599 with a document setting out the Spaniards' intention of invading England and promising support to any Catholics who rallied to them. After being captured by the Portuguese he managed to escape, but then fell into the hands of the Spanish. He was shown some papers by a fellow captive and was able to hide one in his shoes. The man, John Billot of Fowey, persisted in his story of being a Frenchman and was released. He made his way to Morlaix and succeeded in obtaining a place on a Topsham barque. Having arrived at Topsham he went straight to the Mayor of Exeter and showed him the papers, which by now had been translated into English. Although the official accounts set out the tale as factual, it does not ring true and may have been propaganda.

AD 1580 to 1625

4 TUDOR FARMING

As well as being a thriving port, Topsham was home to a sizeable farming community whose lands occupied most of the area between what are now Fore Street and Rydon Lane. The Tudor era was one of great change, and farming was not to escape this. Unfortunately, the developments which took place were not to everyone's advantage.

The enclosures
In the Middle Ages the Lord of the Manor would retain only a portion of his land, the demesne, for his own use. He might lease other parts to feudal tenants or for money (see Book 4). The rest would be farmed by his villagers or be uncultivated waste land. The villagers farmed an open field system which was not permanently fenced nor was the demesne.

The practice of enclosing farmland was probably due to two factors: the reduction in population during the Black Death of 1348, and the growth of the English woollen industry. Many landowners turned from growing crops to the less labour–intensive and more profitable rearing of sheep. Demesne land and, later, areas of common land were enclosed and used for pasture. At first this arrangement worked well, but as the population grew again many labourers were thrown out of work and home. When workers were needed and none were available, the landowner would lease or sell land and stock. This led to the yeoman class, many of whom prospered and lived in comfortable farmhouses set in their own land.

In the South West enclosures were largely completed by the 17th century, having been hastened by the earlier dissolution of

TOPSHAM SAGA - 6

the monasteries and a change in attitude toward farming. During the 16th century personal profit had become the dominant motive. Men became greedy for more land, and their tenants were forced to pay increased rents or get out (note 4). However the only significant enclosure in Topsham was not made until the 1840s but earlier enclosures elsewhere no doubt led to families coming to Topsham.

Fluctuating prices

There were many poor harvests during the 16th century and prices of produce and stock varied accordingly. In 1527 alone the price of wheat more than doubled from 6/– to 13/– a quarter. In 1580 wheat was sold for £1 a quarter in England, in 1623 the price was 52/–. During this time, the price ranged from 7/6 in 1586 to 92/– in 1597. These variations, however, seem to have had little effect on agricultural wages. Between 1547 and 1549, for example, the price of an ox rose from 39/– to 70/–, whereas the average daily payment to an English farm worker increased only from 4d to 5d.

In middle of Elizabeth's reign conditions

7 *A Tudor breakfast and main meal for a merchant.*

28

improved for the labourer. Meat and corn began to fetch a better price, while the cost of wool declined. This made crops and cattle more profitable, and provided more employment. Nevertheless the situation was far from ideal.

Ineffective legislation

Although some, such as Thomas Moore and Edward VI, expressed compassion for the displaced farm worker, most in authority adopted a dispassionate view. The Government soon realised that half–starved demoralised men are unlikely to make good soldiers. There was also the matter of the marauding hordes of beggars who terrorised villages, towns and cities.

Laws were passed in 1489, 1515, 1534 and 1536 to limit sheep farming, but were ignored by most landowners. Later, by an act of Elizabeth I no cottage could be built with less than four acres of land. This not only provided some livelihood, but also a means of existence. Many a poor man kept a cow or pig on this land, and grew vegetables such as cabbages, carrots, melons, parsnips, pumpkins, radishes and turnips. His family would have little if any money for other food, but those living in places like Topsham would have supplemented their diet by capturing seabirds or fishing. Any outside work was likely to have been both part time and seasonal, and the labourer's wife or daughter often added to their meagre income by spinning wool at home.

Continuing plagues

Just as the weather effected crops, disease took its toll of livestock. An illness which the Tudors called 'moryn' killed off many animals. As its victims included cows, sheep, pigs and horses it is highly likely that 'moryn' represented more than a single disease. Tax assessments for 1524–26 mention an allowance for dead stock. No figures are available for Topsham, but it is unlikely that its farms escaped what appears to have been a widespread epidemic. Animals which died included 869 sheep, 8 hogs and 11 cows at Otterton, 12 km to the east, and 303 sheep and 5 cows at Budleigh only 10 km away. The allowance in reducing a farm's value for tax, varied from parish to parish, due to variations in its calculation, differing attitudes on the part of the tax collectors, or both. Some farmers were permitted 1/– for each dead sheep, others 2/–. Similarly, the allowance for bullocks ranged from 3/4 to 6/–, and that for horses from £1 to £1:6:8.

A more businesslike activity
In spite of the many difficulties experienced by landlord, farmer and labourer alike, farming began to be conducted in a more businesslike manner. When corn was grown, the larger fields made harvesting more efficient. More attention was being paid to the care of the land, and a textbook on agriculture appeared in 1523. Seaweed, straw, ferns and stable manure were used as fertilisers and lime and marl (river and other sediment) were also added to the soil. The Tudor era saw also the growth of the middle–man. Produce was no longer sold direct to the consumer, but through shopkeepers and merchants. Grain was also exported, and a profitable trade was to exist from Topsham to France until the onset of the Civil War in 1642.

AD 1580 to 1625

5 MERCHANT FAMILIES

During the Tudor period the landowner's profit became increasingly dependent on the merchant who sold his goods. Although many resented this change, it was not discouraged by their rulers. As a result the successful merchant acquired not only wealth but also influence.

Merchants and monopolies

The less the competition, the greater are the potential gains. Monopolies were frequently granted by Elizabeth I as an economical means of rewarding services rendered. They cost her little, but in return she received duty on any imported or exported goods. Sir Walter Raleigh was one who benefitted considerably from this arrangement. His privileges included a license to import foreign wines, and from 1584 to 1589 to export woollen goods on payment of duty to the Queen. Raleigh was not merely an ingratiating dandified seaman, but a shrewd entrepreneur who had many business interests in Exeter.

Not surprisingly, Raleigh was not popular among the Exeter merchants, who in general preferred a corporate approach to business. One such was Thomas Spicer, a distinguished Exeter citizen who conducted much of his trade through Topsham and who would have been a familiar sight in the town. Spicer, who died in 1600, was one of five brothers, all of whom were Exeter merchants.

The Spicers

Thomas Spicer's earliest traceable ancestor was William de l'Epee. Over generations the name gradually changed to de

There were Spicers living in Exeter from the 11th century and they had lands in Topsham from before 1273. John Spycer (sic) was a merchant of Topsham in the early 16th century. A Thomas Spicer (died c1560) married a daughter of the Pomeroy family. Their children included: Nicholas (d 1612); Thomas (d 1600); and Cristopher (d 1601)

Nicholas Spicer (b 1536, d 1612), married Honor Garland, no children.

Thomas Spicer (d 1600) married the widow of John Sheere, lived in St Martin's parish and had 5 daughters.

Christopher Spicer (d 1601) married Elizabeth Symonds and had 5 sons and 3 daughters. 2nd son was Nicholas Spicer (d 1647).

Nicholas Spicer (b 1581, d 1647) mayor of Exeter, married 1st Joan Horsey and had 11 children. His third son Richard Spicer (b 1617, d 1670) had a son Edward Spicer (d. 1728)

Edward Spicer (b 1659, d 1728) married Katherine Waad of Topsham. He was mayor of Exeter in 1708. This family lived in St Martin's parish but his youngest daughter Anne died in Topsham in 1791, as did his grand-daughter Bridget (d 1772). The children of his 2nd son (Richard b 1692) included William Spicer (d 1788) of Wear House.

William Spicer (b 1733, d October 1788) was a Member of Parliament, High Sheriff of Devon in 1764 and buried in Topsham. The eldest of his three sons by his 1st wife (William d December 1788) was buried in Topsham. The 11 children of William Spicer MP by his 2nd wife were all baptised at Topsham, but the eldest - William Francis Spicer (d 1853) - sold Wear House but was buried in Topsham.

8 *Principal members of the Spicer family.*

AD 1580 to 1625

l'Espee, de l'Espec, de l'Especier, l'Espicier and then Le Spycer. Three Le Spycer brothers came over with William the Conqueror in 1066. One settled in Devon and his family were to serve the West Country and England for generations to come. John Le Spicer, for example, was returned as Exeter's member of parliament on six occasions during the twenty years following 1218. A John Spicer was to be Mayor of Exeter five times between 1352 and 1359. In 1415 a Spicer was present at Agincourt.

The John Spicer who became Mayor of Exeter in 1273 is recorded as living at Weare in Topsham. In 1329 a John le Spicer and his wife Joan purchased property and land in Topsham from John Saundre and his wife Roesia. At various times the Spicers were to own Weare (sic) Park Manor, South Wonford Manor and Winslade House, as well as properties in Exeter. The Spicers were

9 *Wear House in the Tudor period overlooked the river Exe, as it probably appeared before it was rebuilt by the Rodds.*

TOPSHAM SAGA - 6

a rarity in being one of the very few merchant families who had been able to conduct their business over more than one generation.

Thomas Spicer
Mayor of Exeter 1593

Christopher Spicer
(died 1612?)

Thomas Spicer 1580

10 *Spicers' staple marks identifying their goods.*

A staple merchant

By long established law the merchants in certain towns and cities had been granted exclusive rights to the purchase and and sale of staple goods. These Merchants of the Staple such as Thomas Spicer had, subject to paying tax to the Crown, the monopoly in the trading of wool, sheepskin, leather, tin and lead. As illiteracy was the rule, Spicer's merchandise would have been identified by his staple mark. In many respects this was equivalent to the modern trade–mark, but it held also some of the prestige of a coat–of–arms. Like most of his Exeter colleagues and rivals, Spicer's mark was based on the symbol of the wool staple which resembled a '4'.

The Exeter Company of Merchant Adventurers

Despite the benefits he gained from being a merchant of a staple town, Thomas Spicer was a founder member of a rival concern, *The Company of the Govenor Consulls and Societie of Merchantes Adventurers of the Citie of Excester trafiquing with the realme of Fraunce and the dominions of the Frenche Kinge*, established by Royal Charter in 1560.

Thomas Spicer took a leading part in the activities of the Company and was its Governor in 1589. He no doubt prospered as it had the monopoly of trade with France. Whether out of gratitude or self–interest, Thomas was one of the number of members who in 1584 signed the Bond of Association, a pledge to defend Elizabeth I against assassination. The Company guarded its privileges jealously and took action against any usurpers. In 1594 Robert Petter was fined and threatened with imprisonment for importing textiles from Brittany, some in the *Pleasure* of Topsham. That same year the *Pleasure* was used also by Clement Owleborrowe and his son when they attempted to breach the Company's monopoly.

Two years later, the Merchants had to deal with William Tucker who had imported canvas from France in the Topsham vessel, the *Unite*. In its later days the Company was to be threatened from within. In around 1635 the Company decided to reduce its losses due to piracy by sending goods to France only in especially commissioned ships. Presumably this was to ensure a seaworthy vessel as well as a master of skill and spirit. Each merchant was to pay his share of the owner's fee, generally £150. A number of members added false names to the list of shippers, thereby reducing their proportion of the cost. They also induced John Calle of Topsham, who owned a small barque, to enter goods under his name and then to ship them out in his vessel.

In their heyday the Merchant Adventurers financed voyages

of exploration to both China and North America, Thomas Spicer contributing £12:10:0 to Sir Humphrey Gilbert's ill–fated expedition of 1583 to Newfoundland. They also engaged in works of charity and during the famine of 1596 sold grain cheaply to the poor. As time went on, however, the Company's fortunes declined, its activities having been disrupted by both internal and overseas wars. By 1662 its exports were less than ten per cent of those of other Exeter merchants, and one alone conducted more business than the Company. Shortly afterwards the Merchant Adventurers ceased trading.

Thomas Spicer's ships
Few merchants could afford ships of their own. Harry Maunder (mentioned below), for example had only an eighth share in the *Dragon* of Topsham. Similarly Thomas Spicer was part–owner of the *Gyfte of God* and the *Whitt Beare*, but appears to have owned outright the *Mathewe Wynckley* of 25 tuns burden (a Dawlish 'banker') and the 30 tun *Seabright*. Although he had an interest in the Newfoundland fisheries, the activities of the Merchant Adventurers would have been his major concern.

As he traded with lands on both sides of the Atlantic, many different coins would have passed through Thomas's hands. In his day money represented a certain value of silver or gold. He would have been as satisfied by the French *ecu d'or* or the Spanish *ducat* as by the English pound.

Civic duties
The 16th century Spicers distinguished themselves in civic affairs. Only 23 families furnished more than two of the 163 members of the Exeter City Chamber between 1536 and 1603. The Spicers provided six, and a Spicer was mayor on four occasions between 1592 and 1629, Thomas being appointed in

AD 1580 to 1625

1593. Thomas's brother Nicholas twice served as mayor, in 1592 and 1603, and was Sheriff in 1588. Another Nicholas Spicer, one of Thomas's nephews, also became mayor. Two of Thomas's brothers, Christopher and William, were Sheriffs of Exeter in 1595 and 1598 respectively.

Life at home

Thomas Spicer lived in the Exeter parish of St Martin. An impression of his home can be gleaned from the detailed inventories of the estates of Harry Maunder and William Chappell, who died in 1564 and 1579 respectively. Like Spicer, Chappell served both as Governor of the Merchant Adventurers and as mayor. Many regarded the former as more prestigious.

Spicer would have lived comfortably in a house large enough to accommodate family and servants and to entertain distinguished guests. If Maunder's house was typical it would also have included a shop at the front and a warehouse at the back. In the middle there would have been a courtyard with a first–floor gallery. Maunder's house was of four storeys, the uppermost being a gabled loft. The main room, the hall, was on the first floor. Parlours for day to day use were behind the shop and near the main bedroom on the second floor. The hall in Chappell's house contained an iron frame on which hats swords and maces could be hung. The ceiling was of richly carved oak, as were the wainscoting and fitted cupboards. The windows were of stained glass and hung with curtains of red and green silk. Wall hangings of tapestry or painted cloth or canvas often provided further colour. The room would have been lit by candles as well as the fire in the large open hearth. The hall floor would have been carpeted. In many homes, however, carpets were used mainly as table or bed coverings. A large long table dominated the hall. Most of those dining would have sat on cushioned stools or benches, only the head of the house and his wife having chairs. These were often covered by needlework or leather.

In Elizabethan times few families ate off china. The poor used wooden platters or thick slices of bread, but the Spicers' plate would have been of silver or pewter. When not in use it would be displayed on a sideboard, or locked away in one of many boxes and chests. The kitchens of the well–off were amply equipped, most of the utensils being of brass. That of the Chappells possessed a rare luxury, a box of knives. At night Thomas and his wife would have slept in a large curtained bed on a mattress of feather or down. His servants, however, may have had to make do with trestles and straw–filled mattresses.

It was only in the poorer households where the women were expected to add to the family income. The burden of day–to–day expenses would therefore have fallen on Thomas himself. It was not only the Company's books that he had to keep balanced.

The cost of living

Although most households had a bread oven and grew their own vegetables and herbs, as in the 1990s much of the family's food had to be purchased. A comparison with modern prices is difficult, if not impossible. A modern luxury item such as oysters could be bought for 4d a bushel (8 gallons) in 1588, whereas 2lb of marmalade cost 5/–. That same year best mutton sold for three halfpence a pound, best beef costing twice as much. A quail could be purchased for a halfpenny, a chicken for a penny and a goose for a groat.

Should she feel the need for them, the English housewife could buy 200 fresh herrings for 3/–, although keeping so many in her larder was impractical unless they were salted. To go with a meal of herrings, two tankards of beer set the drinker back 1d, but a bottle of Gascony wine was substantially more expensive at 2/–.

The merchant's household included servants. In 1594 the Exeter Quarter Sessions laid down an annual wage of not more than 30/– for a common manservant aged between 16 and 20 years. Those older could receive 40/–. As ever, the women fared less well. Female servants under 14 years of age were allowed meat, drinks and clothes only. During the next four years they could be paid up to 18/– each year, or 12/– plus free clothing. After the age of 18 years the female servant's maximum yearly wage increased to £1:3:4, or 16/8 if clothing was provided. These rates of wages must have influenced the wages paid in Topsham.

A man's world
In spite of being ruled by a woman, or perhaps because of it, the Elizabethan Englishman had things very much his own way. His place was out in the world, and the women's at home. Nevertheless, the dissolution of the nunneries meant that more and more young women were being exposed to not only spiritual but also domestic influences. Narrow as it might have been at first, they were taking a greater interest in the world about them. As Thomas Spicer probably discovered, having five daughters but no son, even the Elizabethan woman had her moments.

6 THE ELIZABETHAN MAID

The Elizabethan girl was born into changing times. The advent of the printing press and the rediscovery of the Americas had done much to broaden men's minds. Throughout Europe the established order was being questioned. The Catholic church had lost its religious authority, and in matters of science and philosophy men were doubting dogma laid down by the ancient Greeks. Elizabethan parenthood would not have been an easy task, and many families opted for robust pragmatism. Discipline could be brutal by modern standards, but tenderness and friendship were equally important when called for.

Tudor learning

The Tudor sovereigns were well–educated and seem to have been determined that their subjects enjoy this privilege. Many presently famed schools were established, but now serve the elite rather than those of ability irrespective of social background. Education, however, was not compulsory, and in the girl in particular would have depended very much on her parents' means and aspirations. Some girls would never read nor write and were taught little other than routine household management by their mothers. On the other hand, daughters of the very rich had their private tutors and became as fluent in Latin, Greek, French, philosophy and mathematics as they were in written and spoken English. In between these extremes, many girls would have received a basic general education from the local dame school or from their vicar.

At home, the Topsham merchant or ship owner might encourage his daughter to become familiar with his trade. If she were to become a merchant's wife she may need to be prepared to take

AD 1580 to 1625

over his affairs during his absence abroad or after his death. Wherever the girl was taught, corporal punishment was often resorted to. Lady Jane Grey, for example, complained bitterly of the many 'pinches, nippes, and bobbes' inflicted on her. Sadly, these were nothing compared to her final punishment. As far as their general behaviour was concerned, girls were expected to be devout in their religion and respectful to their betters. In many families children had to kneel when in their parents' presence.

Games, pastimes and accomplishments

Many of the Elizabethan child's toys and games are still enjoyed. All but the poorest girl had a doll, and most boys a pop–gun and drum. Skipping, top–spinning, blind–man's buff and hide and seek have all stood the test of time, but such games as figgans, mosel–the–pigge (muzzle–the–pig?) and playing for the hole about the church–yard, are now known only by name. As the girl grew older she would have learned card games, most of which resembled modern whist, and board games such as chess, draughts, backgammon and Nine–men's Morris. However, her parents might have frowned upon the many games of chance involving dice.

11 *Tudor playing cards.*

Needlework, archery and dancing were important accomplishments for the Elizabethan maiden. Skill with needle and thread had practical as well as recreational value, and a number of pattern books became available toward the end of the 16th century. The page would be placed over the material and the pattern pricked through with a pin. Powdered charcoal or cuttlefish bone would then be dusted through the holes leaving a neat outline to follow. Archery included the use of the crossbow as well as the traditional longbow, and almost every town and village had their butts where the young and old of both sexes could practice, in Topsham on what in the 1990s is Bowling Green Marsh.

Most balls began with the solemn steps of the minuet, corrando or galliard and our girl would be expected to learn their steps. It would, however, be the dances later in the evening that she would enjoy most. The cushion dance, also called Joan Sanderson or prinkum prankum, was particularly popular, as was the Frenchmore in which the dancers formed a line. By the end of the night all would be dancing together — master and servant, lady and kitchen–maid.

Bread, beef and beer

Those living in Topsham would have a ready supply of fish, meat, wild and domesticated fowl, fruit, vegetables, dairy products and cereals, and the girl's diet would have been reasonably balanced. However, fresh produce was not always available and during certain seasons salted, smoked or pickled food would have to be used. Cooking was over an open fire, but there was usually a small recess on one side for baking bread. A typical breakfast of the merchant's family would have been bread and butter, eggs and broiled beef steak, all washed down with a cup or two of ale. For the less well off breakfast would have been bread with cheese or dripping. Dinners were elaborate and consisted of three or four courses. Meat was more fashionable than fish, brawn (seasoned jellied loaf from pig's head) being a popular dish among all classes, but in Elizabethan times laws were passed to forbid the eating of meat on various weekdays and in Lent. This was to bolster the fishing industry and the seafaring towns. Merchants and farmers dined around noon. The gentry tended not to rise for breakfast, but dined an hour earlier. The Elizabethans enjoyed music and singing and a family entertainment might follow dinner or supper. Supper usually consisted of cold meat, cheese and wine or ale. Before retiring a snack would be taken consisting often of fruit and sack (a dry white sherry–like wine).

Many households would have considered this diet too rich for a child. In keeping with then medical theories, many children had to make do with milk, cream, whey, curds and white meat or fish.

Long hair, loose skirts, tight bodices and show–offs
The young girl wore her hair long and hanging down the back. As she grew older she might have it cut short or frizzened at the sides in tight crisp curls. If the hair was kept long it would be worn high and widened at the top. A girl wishing to be especially fashionable would dye her hair red to imitate the queen's.

Skirts were long and full, and worn over a chemise and fringed petticoat. On formal occasions and if following London fashion, the petticoat would be a hooped farthingale or the skirt would be further extended at the hips by bumrolls. The bodice was usually worn tight, but the sleeves were puffed and had high wings. Unmarried women did not wear hats. When on their way to the Saturday market Topsham girls such as Joan Tooslow and Hester Ellet might wear a chin–clout. This was a square of material worn over the chin in many country districts and served to protect from dust and wind.

The Elizabethans had a habit of wearing their wealth. The more prosperous the family, the more richly was the dress decorated. A Puritan minority, however, deplored such ostentation. Others also disliked this practice, but for different reasons. The rise of the merchant and yeoman classes did much for England's prestige and prosperity, but alarmed those who wished to see the established social order preserved. Between 1559 and 1597 some ten proclamations were issued in an attempt to prevent people dressing above their station. For example petticoats made of velvet, tufted taffeta and satin could be worn only by the wives of barons, knights or councillors, ladies of the Privy Chamber and Maids of Honour. These regulations, however, appear to have been largely ignored and hardly ever enforced.

A pale and natural complexion
A pale complexion had been fashionable for long before Elizabeth came to the throne, but it was in her reign that this was first achieved by cosmetics rather than just shielding the face from the sun. However, some of the white face powders did more harm than good as they were based on poisonous white lead. Similarly, rouge used on the cheeks sometimes contained mercury. By contrast lipstick, which was based on powdered alabaster or plaster of Paris, and ointments containing asses milk, honey or lard were much safer. After being applied, the make–up was usually protected by a thin glaze of egg white (note 5).

In her declining years Queen Elizabeth was said to apply half–an–inch thickness of cosmetics and would paint veins on her forehead to make the skin look translucent. Younger women sometimes painted false veins on their breasts. Hopefully, the Topsham girl had no time for such vanity. She was more than content if her face withstood weather and disease. The chin–clout offered some protection when out and about, and a mask might also be worn.

AD 1580 to 1625

Health and hygiene
Although it was expected that the hands would be washed before meals and the teeth regularly cleansed, most of the rest of the body received scant attention. Baths were seldom taken unless to keep warm in winter or ease the pain of arthritis. One author recommended that the hair be washed about four times a year using a mixture of wood ash and water. Not surprisingly perfumes, often made in the home, were used as deodorants and not to arouse the desires of men.

Courtship
Unlike in Commonwealth and Victorian times, open affection was not frowned upon. It was quite acceptable to kiss and fondle in public, and at social gatherings the man would make no secret of his feelings and lie or sit at his lady's feet gazing into her eyes. Playing with the little finger and kissing on the eyes were thought of as marks of special tenderness. It was considered particularly gallant for the young man to drink to his beloved's health in urine.

Tokens of love, such as a plaited lock of hair which the man would hang from his left ear, were displayed freely. He might wear also one of his lady's scarves hung loosely over his clothes or tied around a sleeve. The clothes themselves would be untidy to demonstrate his preoccupation with more heartfelt matters. Letters would be exchanged and the girl would keep her's tucked close to her bosom. The bodice would sometimes be worn loose so that her lover could place them there himself. The most hoped for sign of love, however, was the ring that marked betrothal.

The Wedding procession
The Elizabethans relished pageant and ceremony, and every possible festival was enjoyed to the full. Weddings were no exception. As in the 1990s the bride held pride of place. Her dress

was often brightly coloured and ornamented with gold thread. A bride–cup adorned with gilded sprigs of rosemary and hung with silver ribbons was borne before her, and she would be led by two bachelors wearing bride–lace and rosemary on their sleeves. The groom was escorted also by young men, but they would have green broom from a shrub on their arms. A party of musicians followed, and then young maidens carrying bride–cakes and garlands of finely gilded wheat. The path to the church was often strewn with herbs, flowers and rushes, and to add to the fragrance the guests carried nosegays. The ceremony usually commenced at the church door but was completed at the altar, a veil then being draped over both bride and groom. The festivities began in the church with the guests drinking from the bride–cup and eating cakes. As the bride left, young men would vie to be the first to remove her garters and place them in their hats. To prevent any indecorousness the ribbons on the bride's legs were deliberately tied loosely.

Future hopes
Gifts were freely distributed to guests and those unable to attend, and were worn pinned on the sleeve, breast or hat. The young women would remove their pins at the first opportunity after the wedding, believing that this hastened their own marriage.

AD 1580 to 1625

7 THE POOR AND THE LAW

The development of the enclosure system resulted in labourers losing their work and many tenants their homes. Also the dissolution of the monasteries not only accelerated the change in how land was managed, but meant that the poor could no longer turn to the monks and nuns.

Topsham charity
Whether in Catholic or Protestant days the inhabitants of Topsham would have seen giving to the poor as a natural Christian duty. Some would have set aside money for this, others would have been content to pay their tithe and leave the matter to the church. Money would also be bequeathed. Thus in 1592 John Elsdon left 40/– 'to the poor men's box of Topsham'. Perhaps conscience prompted John Ralegh (sic) to leave £3 to St Margaret's Church 'for tithing and offerings forgotten by me' in his will of 1501. A similar bequest of 10/– was made in 1524 by Mathew Mongey, whose father had witnessed Raleigh's will. In 1600 John Watkins left the rent of a house in Exeter, later the King's Head Inn, to the poor of Topsham, and in 1613 Sir John Acland of Cullumjohn was to give £10 towards the apprenticeship of four poor Topsham children. Also John Shere left four High Street houses (possibly in modern Fore Street) for the benefit of the poor in 1636.

The growth of the Poor Laws
The Tudor governments may have been the first in England to have to cope with mass unemployment, but they were certainly not the last. Their approach was based on two principles. Beggars

who were capable of work should be made to work. Secondly, those who could not work should be cared for in almshouses or hospitals.

By an early Act of 1501, Justices of the Peace were entrusted with the punishment of the sturdy beggar. The 1531 Poor Law drew a distinction between able beggars unsuccessfully seeking work and those who were work–shy. The Justices could have the latter whipped, but were also empowered to give licenses to the former. In 1536 the penalties for unlawful vagrancy were made more severe. People found begging and though able to work, were still to be whipped, but only for their first offence. Ear clipping was the penalty for the next conviction, and hanging followed the third. As to those unable to work, the Parishes were made responsible for the collection of alms and the provision of care. An Act of 1547 removed the death penalty. Instead, vagrants could be branded with a letter V and enslaved for two years. Persistent offenders were branded with the letter S and became slaves for life. By contrast, the same Act ordered local authorities to find houses to lodge the sick, the old and the incapable. However, such accommodation depended on charity and was not easily provided.

12 *A vagrant of Tudor times.*

An Act of 1563 imposed sanctions on those who refused to give to collections for the poor, but the amount remained up to the individual. This voluntary element was removed in 1572 when the Justices were empowered to set the size of contributions. The relief of the poor thus became an imposed tax. Masterless men still had to reside in their own parish, but by the Act of 1572 those such as bear–minders and strolling actors could be given a license to travel. There was still the matter of giving the poor employment whenever possible. An Act of 1576 authorised the setting up of Houses of Industry where the poor could work with material provided by the parish. There were also to be Houses of Correction where the indolent could be sent. However, in practice little was done in this respect for some 25 years.

In 1598 the responsibility for administering the poor rate passed from the Justices to the Parish Churchwardens and an Overseer. To reduce the burden of having to care for those from elsewhere, the parish constables were authorised to summarily whip incoming vagrants and then return them to their parish of origin. The Poor Law of 1601 consolidated previous legislation and attempted to place it on a systematic national footing. The parish was to be responsible for the care of the helpless, and this was to be financed by a compulsory levy of 1d a week administered by the Overseer. Secondly, unemployment was to be relieved at the expense of the parish by the provision of work materials and the apprenticeship of the young pauper. Finally, the incorrigible were to be punished by the Justices. From 1603 parishioners could absolve themselves from further contributions to the poor rate by making a lump–sum payment of £2. Thomas Maiser was one of the first to do so in Topsham. Penalties were introduced for those Overseers who misappropriated funds, the fine of £3:6:8 being evenly divided between the informant and the poor.

Although the poor were to continue to cause concern, and still do, in essence little was to change until the Poor Law Amendment

Act of 1834. Acts of 1662 and 1697 clarified the position of the pauper labourer, and granted him more mobility. A 'poor wandering ballad maker' known only as Mary was buried in Topsham in 1673, as was a journeyman shoemaker 'a stranger' two years later. By 1723 parish work schemes had deteriorated and many of the poor were being housed in rented cottages. An Act of that year encouraged the setting up of residential workhouses, that of Topsham being built in Follett Road. But there were many acts of charity in these centuries, some examples of which are shown in note 6.

Municipal initiatives

Many of the more progressive City Chambers pre–empted the measures of the 1601 and earlier Acts. Records for 1563 show that Exeter had a system whereby citizens paid a predetermined poor rate. The assessments could be as low as a farthing each week and rarely exceeded 4d. In that year £119 was spent on the poor. In 1597 the Exeter Quarter Sessions directed every householder to be assigned one or more poor to be given two meals a day. Alternatively, they could pay 18d per week. The parishes were searched regularly for vagrants, who after punishment would be sent back to their birth place or wherever they had spent most of the previous three years. These practices in the City may have influenced Topsham's poor rate, although Exeter was exceptional among cities at this time, in its care for the poor.

Discharges

People moving home from one parish to another would often carry a discharge with them. This was a statement that the first parish would have them back should they become destitute, and would be kept carefully in the parish chest. The oldest one noted for Topsham is dated 23 January 1675 and concerns a Joan Smith

AD 1580 to 1625

who came there from Lympstone. There is also a record of a Margaret Squire and her two children being discharged from Topsham to Kenn in 1690.

There are many examples of matters not proceeding smoothly for either the vagrant or the authorities. In 1683 a party of Irish vagrants arrived at Topsham and had to be sent back after each received a whipping. In 1723 the Constable had to remove a beggar pretending to have been a Barbary captive. One Mary Swaffin was found to be stealing food from the workhouse in 1739 and had also to be dealt with. The disorderly behaviour of those leaving the workhouse on the pretext of going to church led in 1744 to them not being allowed out on weekdays. In July 1747 the Parish Committee inspected the poor in case any were suffering due to greed and lack of affection on the part of their keepers.

Finding work for the poor was not easy, and in 1758 white rope making was abandoned as too costly and of no benefit to the town. By the early 1800s the Topsham poor were being kept occupied in sorting rags and unpicking oakum (old caulking rope). In 1829 it was suggested that the wasteland by Topsham Bridge be enclosed to provide agricultural work, but nothing seems to have come of this. Meanwhile the workhouse had acquired an unsavoury reputation. By the 1820s the workhouse had acquired an unsavoury reputation. Francis Davy, by no means an inhumane man, called it 'that costly nest of vice and dissipation'. In 1825 orders were made for its closure. Clara Place now marks its site.

Appendix I: Chronology

1581	Another commission sits to consider ways of suppressing piracy.
1582	In October the *Whitt Beare* (*White* [Polar] *Bear*) sails from the Exe for Newfoundland, one of the few early ships to cross the Atlantic in winter.
1583	Exeter merchants support Sir Humphrey Gilbert's voyage to set up colony in Newfoundland
1584	English ships can only provide about a third of fish required, 10 years later this fell to a tenth.
1584	Plymouth put a tax on pilchards landed, to pay for their harbour defences.
1585	Trade with Constantinople despite war with Spain until 1604.
1585	War with Spain, ends 1604.
1586	Nine ships of Topsham in Newfoundland trade in this period.
1587	Exeter Chamber repair Town Quay.
1588	Apsam ships sail against the Armada.
1589	Three stone–boats in customs' rolls for Exeter
1589	English merchants expelled from Lisbon.
1600	Trade with Mediterranean from the Exe estuary.
1600	The first insurance policies to cover fishing ships, reduced rates of interest on money to finance them.
1600	Coal from Wales and Newcastle upon Tyne becomes a major import to southern England after this year.
1600	John Wattlings (sic) leaves house in Exeter worth £60 to Topsham poor, it later became Exeter's King's Head.
1600	Narrow wooden bridge exists across the Clyst east of Bridge' Hill.
1601	Poor Relief Act requires parish to take over all charities for the poor, and stipulates beneficiaries.
1603	Queen Elizabeth dies aged 68 years and is succeeded by James I (James VI of Scotland).
1607	Exeter Chamber lease Town Quay for four years.
1620	Pilgrim Fathers reach Plymouth (Maine).
1624	War with Spain, not concluded till 1630.
1625	Death of James I, Charles I comes to the throne.

AD 1580 to 1625

Appendix II: Notes and summary of sources

1. The dates are those of the calendar used in England in 1588. Since 1582 Catholic Europe had been using the Gregorian calendar, which was ten days ahead. The days of the week, however, were the same. By 1582 the Julian calendar (which had begun on 1 January 45 BC) was lagging ten days behind the solar calendar. Pope Gregory XIII therefore ruled that 5 October of that year should become 15 October. England, however, did not alter its calendar until 1752 when 3 September became 14 September. At the same time, the official start of the new year was changed from 25 March to 1 January, but the government made 6 April the start of the fiscal year, reportedly so as not to lose 11 day's worth of taxes.

2. The Dutch 'Sea Beggars' were ships owned and manned by Protestant exiles from the Netherlands. They had an implacable hatred of Spain and frequently attacked her ships. One of Elizabeth's less popular acts of diplomacy barred them from using English ports.

3. Fire-ships were steered by one man who would light the trails of pitch and then leap aside at the last minute to swim for the small boat following his ship. In 1585 a single fire-ship had caused the deaths of 1,000 Spaniards.

4. At the end of the 16th century it was written that: Sheep have eaten up our meadows and our downs; Our corn, our wood, whole villages and towns. T. Bastard (1566–1618).

5. A pale round face with a high forehead and pink dimpled cheeks was highly thought of. The eyebrows were kept thin and pencilled in, the lips were painted coral pink or cherry red. Small, rounded ears were thought attractive as was a round, white pillar-like neck. The shoulders of the fashionable figure were wide; the breasts high, fair and round; the waist narrow and the hips broad. Small white hands with red nails and small feet were desirable.

– continued

TOPSHAM SAGA - 6

Appendix II: continued

6. Many records exemplify the charitable work carried out by the Topsham Overseers of the Poor during the two centuries and more before the 1601 Poor Law was amended. On 25 October 1713 a child found in a basket in Monmouth St was baptised John Topsham and 5/– per month given for his upkeep. A male baby found in Lime Street in 1808 was also given the name Topsham. More imaginatively a baby found in George Clapp's carpenters yard on 14th February 1820, was named George Valentine Carpenter. In 1723 Ann Beavis was given 1/– after her chimney had fallen in. In 1736 two women were paid to sit with the dying Sarah Strickland and Jane Pym received 10/– for caring for the sick wife of a soldier. The widow and young children of Thomas Burrow were granted 16/– each month in 1785 while waiting for his will to be proved. If she inherited, the parish was to be repaid. In 1797 the Overseer paid for Mr Norton's herring net to be enlarged and repaired. The town also operated a form of legal aid. In 1781 a fund was set up to enable the poor to pursue actions against thieves and trespassers. It was not only Topsham people who were helped. Two castaway Frenchmen received 6d in 1723, and in the same year Mary Annford and her young child were given 1/– to help them continue on their way to London.

Sources: The principle primary sources are various papers and publications held in the Devon Record Office, the Devon and Exeter Institution and the Exeter Central Reference Library. The major secondary sources have been the Transactions of the Devonshire Association and Devon and Cornwall Notes and Gleanings. (See Book 22.)

ACKNOWLEDGEMENTS

Gratitude is owed to the Topsham Museum Society and in particular to their President, Mrs Barbara Entwistle MBE, and the Committee Chairman, Mrs Cathy Maguire. Many thanks are due also to James D. Ladd for his unfailing support and guidance over the author's transition from medical to historical writing. Without the enthusiasm and technical skills of his partner in Apsam Books, Peter Melhuish: rough notes on the backs of envelopes would never have been transmuted into print.

The author is grateful to the librarians and staff of the Topsham Library, the Exeter Central Library, the Devon and Exeter Institution, the West Country Studies Centre, the Devon Record Office, the Manchester Central Library and the Etobicoke Public Library (Toronto) — to them all, for their unstinted courtesy, patience and assistance. I am also most grateful for the help of many individuals who have commented on the draft text or otherwise assisted me, including: Patricia Lee, Dr John Allan curator of antiquities at the Royal Albert Memorial Museum of Exeter, the staff of the Exeter Museums Archaeological Field Unit, Mr 'Bob' Harvey and Mrs Ann Harding.

Finally, a debt is due to those previous researchers into the history of Topsham such as the Holmans, the Davys, Nicholas Brand, Dr F.W. Ross, W.J. Bridle, H. Stone and H. Tapley–Soper for making the results of their labours available for future generations.

TOPSHAM SAGA - 6

WHO? Apsam Books is a small publishing house owned by James D. Ladd and Peter W. Melhuish. PWM is a lecturer in Computer Studies at Plymouth University and has his own computing facilities on which these publications have been made. Dr Sadru Bhanji has written a number of medical papers, a book and articles on the history of psychiatry. The Saga Books have been illustrated by Jan M. Rogers who is a professional artist, well-known for her paintings of flowers and who has worked on cartography for the Department of the Environment.

When? The saga of Topsham's history is in 22 books to which a number of authors are contributing. Books 1 to 12 cover the chronological history of life in this town from the time of the first settlers here in about 4000 BC to the late 20th century, set against the background of English history. The remainder of the series show particular aspects of this saga which are linked to the chronological books through the index in Book 21. (Book 22 sets out the sources of information in the books.)

Where? Topsham in the 1990s is a suburb of Exeter and was for many centuries that city's port. As a town in its own right before 1966, it was a busy port with increasing trade until the 1750s, which was its most prosperous decade. Its seafarers traded and fought in many distant waters including Newfoundland, the Mediterrean and the Baltic. (The town included Countess Wear as does this saga.)

Topsham can be reached by car: M5 motorway junction 30, turn south on A376 (the Exmouth road) through Clyst Saint Mary to Clyst St George and turn west. Alternatively: from Exeter take the Topsham Road south for 3 km through Countess Wear's major roundabout and in another 3 km enter Topsham. Visitors may also come by train: Mainline Exeter St David's or Central, and service to Topsham.